HEROD THE GREAT

HEROD THE GREAT

BY
ROBERT GREEN

A FIRST BOOK

FRANKLIN WATTS
A DIVISION OF GROLIER PUBLISHING
NEW YORK – LONDON – HONG KONG – SYDNEY
DANBURY, CONNECTICUT

For D.R. Green

Cover design by Robin Hoffmann
Cover photograph copyright ©: The Bridgeman Art Library

Map by MacArt Design
Photographs copyright ©: The Bridgeman Art Library, frontis, p. 24; Art Resource, NY:
pp. 8, 26, 43, 44, 50, 57 (all Erich Lessing), 10 (Foto Marburg), 38 (Giraudon); The
Bettmann Archive: pp. 16, 22, 34; Photo Researchers: pp. 20 (Sylvain Grandadam),
46 (Gordon Gahan), 46 inset (Mark D. Phillips); University of Pennsylvannia
Museum, Philadelphia: p. 29 (Giorgio Sommer); Hulton Deutsch Collection: pp. 32,
40, 52; North Wind Picture Archives: p. 55.

Library of Congress Cataloging-in-Publication Data

Green, Robert.
Herod the Great / by Robert Green.
p.   cm. — (A First Book)
Includes bibliographical references and index.
ISBN 0-531-20232-1 (lib. bdg.)—ISBN 0-531-15801-2 (pbk.)
1. Herod I, King of Judea, 73–4 B.C. 2. Jews—History—168 B.C.–135 A.D.
3. Jews—Kings and rulers—Biography.   I. Title.   II. Series.
DS122.3.G67   1996
933'.05'092—dc20   95-26327 CIP AC
[B]

CONTENTS

He stole along to the throne like a fox,
He ruled like a tiger, and he died like a dog.
—JOSEPHUS, JEWISH HISTORIAN

THE YOUNG WARRIOR

The Bible speaks of a king named Herod who was cruel and jealous. According to St. Matthew, a group of wise men came to Jerusalem during Herod's reign to see the newborn Jesus Christ. When Herod received them, they asked, "Where is he who has been born king of the Jews? For we have seen his star in the East, and have come to worship him."

The words of the wise men threw Herod into a rage. Who would dare call himself king of the Jews, when Herod, though old and dying, was still king? He sent his soldiers to seek out all the children two years old and younger in the village of Bethlehem and in all the nearby towns and farms. He wanted to find this child they called the king of the Jews. But an angel of

The three wise men appearing before Herod

the Lord appeared to Joseph, the father of Jesus, and said, "Rise, take the child and his mother, and flee to Egypt, and remain there till I tell you; for Herod is about to search for the child, to destroy him."

Joseph followed the advice and escaped with Jesus and Mary. Meanwhile, Herod slaughtered all the other children in Bethlehem and the surrounding areas, hoping that Jesus was among them.

According to the story, Herod died a short time later. Then the angel of the Lord again appeared to Joseph and said, "Rise, take the child and his mother, and go to the land of Israel, for those who sought the child's life are dead."

ACCORDING TO MATTHEW

This story is called the Slaughter of the Innocents. There is no evidence that it really happened, but it is recorded in the Gospel of Matthew, the first of the three synoptic Gospels of the New Testament. Each of the authors of the synoptic Gospels—Matthew, Mark, and Luke—provided an outline, or synopsis, of the life and teachings of Jesus Christ. Matthew's Gospel was written sometime between A.D. 70 and 100. As an early Christian, probably living in the Roman province of Syria, Matthew had broken with the ancient religion of the Jews in order to follow the teachings of Christ.

The traditional, or orthodox, Jewish religion was being challenged by the followers of Christ. Christians would come to view the New Testament as a vital part of the Bible, while the Jews recognized only the Old Testament as authentic spiritual and historical record. Matthew's account of the Slaughter of the Innocents illustrates just how much the Jews, traditional or radical, despised King Herod after his death. They hated Herod for many reasons, but perhaps mostly because he was a foreigner and because his cruelty was so severe that it won him notoriety and loathing even in a time when cruelty was common. The Gospel of Matthew recorded the indignities suffered by the Jews under Herod for later generations to remember.

King Herod, whose name is inscribed in Italian at the top of this relief sculpture, is presented with a slaughtered Jewish child. The Book of Matthew tells of Herod slaughtering the children of Judea to prevent the coming of Christ, who some prophesied to be the future king of the Jews.

JUDEA

In Herod's time, the country that is known today as Israel consisted of smaller tribal regions. The Bible refers to these lands as Judea, Samaria, Galilee, Edom (also called Idumaea), and a handful of other names. For centuries these tribes were in the kingdoms of Judah and ancient Israel. The people from Judea expanded their territory and eventually became dominant over the region that is today roughly the same as modern Israel. In this book, the region will simply be called Judea, as it was often called in biblical times.

Jerusalem was the capital of Judea and its most important city. It was the center of both religion and politics. The city's leader was the high priest and the king of the Jews. Religion and politics were not divided in ancient Judea as they are in Israel today. The position of high priest was passed from father to son in a royal family, or dynasty. Before Herod rose to power, the family that ruled Judea was called the Hasmonean dynasty.

During the reign of the Hasmonean king and high priest John Hyrcanus, from 134 to 104 B.C., the Jews conquered Idumaea, the land south of Judea. Idumaea was inhabited at the time by an Arab tribe. The Bible refers to this land as Edom and its people as Edomites.

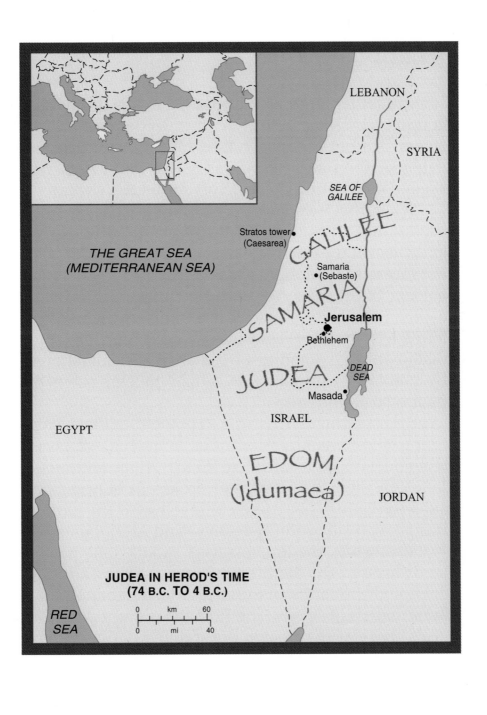

LEBANON

SYRIA

SEA OF
GALILEE

Stratos tower
(Caesarea)

GALILEE

THE GREAT SEA
(MEDITERRANEAN SEA)

Samaria
(Sebaste)

SAMARIA

Jerusalem

Bethlehem

JUDEA

DEAD
SEA

Masada

ISRAEL

EGYPT

EDOM
(Idumaea)

JORDAN

RED
SEA

**JUDEA IN HEROD'S TIME
(74 B.C. TO 4 B.C.)**

| 0 | km | 60 |
| 0 | mi | 40 |

HEROD'S FAMILY

Herod's father, Antipater, lived in Idumaea during the conquest by King John Hyrcanus. Under the Jewish rulers, Antipater converted to Judaism and had his family do the same. Herod was born about 74 B.C., the second son of Antipater and his Arab wife, Cypros.

When the Jews conquered Idumaea, they probably did not expect an Arab to become a powerful influence on the Hasmonean kings. They certainly did not foresee the blood-thirsty Herod one day becoming king of the Jews. Yet Herod's family used the Hasmonean occupation of Idumaea to insert themselves into Jewish politics. They moved closer and closer to taking power, sometimes by chance and sometimes by cunning. Eventually they would become rulers of their own conquerors.

Herod's grandfather was appointed military governor of Idumaea by Alexander Jannaeus, who was Hasmonean king from 103 to 76 B.C. When Alexander Jannaeus died, in 76, civil war broke out between his sons Hyrcanus (not to be confused with the earlier Hasmonean king John Hyrcanus) and Aristobulus.

Meanwhile, the Romans were rapidly taking over lands around the Mediterranean Sea. They already occupied the lands of Syria (modern Lebanon and Syria) north of Judea. The Romans did not want Judea's civil war to threaten the stability of the region.

CIVIL UNREST

In 63 B.C. the Roman general Pompey marched his soldiers from Syria to the gates of Jerusalem. The Romans put Aristobulus in chains and took him to Rome. There he was paraded in Triumph (a formal celebration of a Roman victory) in front of the cheering Romans. Hyrcanus was appointed high priest. But the real victor of the civil war was Herod's father, Antipater, who had won the favor of the Romans.

Rome was fighting its own civil war at the same time. When Julius Caesar defeated Pompey, Antipater allied himself with Caesar. Caesar repaid Antipater by making him a citizen of Rome and appointing him governor of Judea. Antipater was an Arab and therefore unsuited to be high priest, so Hyrcanus kept that position. For the first time in Judea, religious and political powers were separated. But Antipater's government ruled the country, and it was backed by the foreign power Rome.

Antipater dreamed of great glories for his sons. He made Herod governor of Galilee, the land to the north of Judea and Samaria. Soon after, when the Jews of Galilee revolted against the new Arab ruler, Herod had a chance to prove himself in battle. He was twenty-six years old, tall, strong, and cunning. He and his troops rode fiercely after the rebels. They slaughtered one after another, then ruthlessly hunted the

Although defeated by Julius Caesar in the Roman Civil War, Pompey, like Herod, carried the title Magnus, or "great," in recognition of his years of military service to Rome, especially in the eastern provinces.

rebel leader, Ezekias, captured and tortured him, and put him to death.

Ezekias and his group were branded as outlaws by Herod because they refused to pay the taxes and obey the laws of the Herodian administration. Mainstream Jews, although not always willing to risk their lives like Ezekias, usually sympathized with the rebels. The traditional Jewish government allowed for no separation between church and state. Before Herod and the Romans reduced the power of the church, the Jewish religion dictated the spiritual and legal responsibilities of Jews. Many, therefore, viewed the Jewish brigands as patriots, fighting for a return to a nation run not by foreigners but by Judaic law.

THE SANHEDRIN

The Jews did not forget the ruthlessness with which Herod crushed the revolt. His enemies used his success against him. They claimed that he had no right to murder the rebellious Jews, who were religious fanatics and, therefore, protected under religious law. The Sanhedrin, the Jewish high court, summoned Herod to answer for his actions.

Life or death could be decided by the Sanhedrin. Trials there were very serious affairs. In general, those appearing before the Sanhedrin humbled themselves, showing respect for the judges in order to make a good impression. But not Herod. He arrived with armed bodyguards and wore splendid, colorful clothing. He then strode into the courts with the bearing of royalty and a look of defiance. This did much to darken Herod's prospects, for the judges were already resentful of the Arab influence in Judea.

Herod most certainly would have been convicted of slaughtering the Jewish rebels. All of a sudden, though, word came from Rome that Herod was not to be found guilty. He left the court chambers triumphant. The Herod about whom the Bible speaks, the cruel and arrogant king, was emerging, with the help of Rome.

2

THE CLIENT KING

Herod's family was more willing to cooperate with Rome than were the Hasmonean royal family or the Jewish people themselves. The Herodians—as Herod's family members were called—were Jews by religion but Arabs by blood. The Jews were very worried, because they knew that the Herodian leaders were destroying traditional Jewish government.

Rome chose Herod's family as rulers for Judea in order to avoid the intricacies of the Jewish religious government. Also, with the Herodians in charge, no one would be able to rise up in protest against Rome. The Herodians were nothing without Rome. Rome could, therefore, count on extreme loyalty from them.

In Herod's time, Jerusalem was truly an international city. This photograph shows the churches, mosques, and temples of the Old City as well as the modern buildings of West Jerusalem (the New City). The spectacular blue building in the foreground is the Dome of the Rock, a Muslim mosque built in the seventh century A.D. to house the rock from which Mohammed supposedly ascended into heaven. The mosque rests on the Temple Mount, which was the site of the great Temple built by Herod.

The Herodians kept a close eye on Roman politics and were careful about forming alliances. When Caesar was assassinated, in 44 B.C., Antipater waited cautiously for a new Roman leader to emerge. Cassius and Brutus had led the group that killed Caesar. Marc Antony and Octavius sought to avenge Caesar's murder. Cassius appealed to Judea for money to finance a war against Marc Antony and Octavius.

Antipater agreed, having little choice. He ordered each of his governors to raise a portion of the funds through taxation. The Judeans resented Antipater for the new taxes and for his method of raising them—by whip and sword.

One tax collector, named Malichus, refused to raise his portion of the taxes for Cassius's army. Malichus was afraid of Antipater, but he hoped to make Antipater look bad by not raising the money. Antipater and Cassius were furious at him and came close to executing him.

Hyrcanus suddenly took pity on Malichus and paid Antipater and Cassius to stop the execution. At a feast, shortly after all the taxes had been collected, Antipater drank from a goblet of poisoned wine and died. The rumor was that Malichus killed Antipater in revenge for the way Antipater and Cassius had treated him. Herod's father had been killed, but this act caused Roman commanders to become more sympathetic to Herod.

RETALIATION

Herod fumed with the desire to avenge his father's death. Hearing of the poisoning, Cassius ordered Roman soldiers to strike down the assassin, thus saving Herod the trouble. Cassius's action secured Herod's supremacy in Judea.

As soon as Herod's friendship with Cassius was strengthened, Marc Antony and Octavius defeated Cassius in 42 B.C. Cassius abandoned hope and threw himself on his sword. Marc Antony, with this victory, became ruler of the eastern half of the Roman lands.

Meanwhile, Herod and the high priest Hyrcanus were attacked by Jewish armies. Herod quickly defeated the rebelling armies.

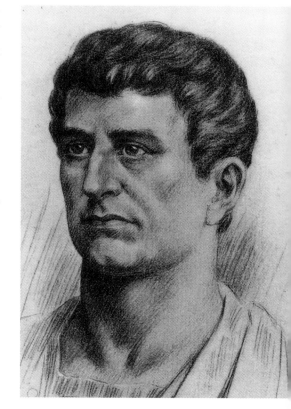

Marc Antony shared an appetite for pleasure and an interest in Hellenism with Herod.

As a reward for his services, Hyrcanus presented to Herod his granddaughter, Mariamme. Herod was already married to an Arab woman named Doris, but marriage to more than one wife was not against the law. In fact, political marriages were common, and Herod could easily see the value of being married to a Hasmonean princess. He agreed to take Mariamme as a wife.

In his lifetime, Herod took at least ten wives and probably fathered twelve or thirteen children. But Doris and Mariamme dominated his life, and the children of these marriages play a big part in Herod's story. By Mariamme he had two children, Alexander and Aristobulus. These two were considered royal princes of the Hasmonean line. By Doris he had a son, Antipater.

Although Antipater was the eldest of the three sons, Alexander and Aristobulus enjoyed more of Herod's attentions. Herod sent Antipater to the Judean countryside to live a quiet life. He sent Alexander and Aristobulus to Rome to learn about politics.

ALLIANCE WITH ROME

Herod was working to maintain his own power and hoping to establish a dynasty through his sons. In order to stay in power, he had to win the favor of Marc Antony, the new leader of the eastern Roman

Antony fought a war against Octavius for control of the Roman territories. His war efforts and his extravagant lifestyle were financed by Cleopatra, seen here disembarking from one of her splendid ships to meet him.

power. But Herod's enemies sent ambassadors to convince Antony to throw Herod out of Judea and restore the traditional Hasmonean dynasty.

Herod hurried to Antony to plead his own case, but he had nothing to worry about. Antony assured Herod he was an ally and a friend. Although Herod had supported Cassius, Antony knew this reflected his devotion to Roman power in the east and not a personal relationship with Cassius.

Both Antony and Herod liked the good life. They loved feasts and wine. Like Herod, Antony was temperamental and given to outbursts of passion. Sometimes he was very generous, but other times he could be very cruel. Antony slaughtered the Jews that were against Herod. He appointed Herod and his elder brother, Phasael, joint rulers of all of Judea. This robbed Hyrcanus of his power and made him nothing more than a puppet controlled by the other two.

NEW ATTACKS ON HEROD

As soon as Herod had won the support of Antony, war broke out again. One of Rome's great enemies, the kingdom of Parthia (modern Iran and part of Iraq), invaded Roman Syria in 40 B.C. and drove the Roman legions west. In all the confusion, the Jews struck at Herod through a powerful leader named Antigonus. Antigonus promised the Parthians rule of Judea in

return for their help in driving Herod out. Just as Herod had found a powerful ally in the Romans, Antigonus established an alliance with the Parthians.

When the Parthians moved into Jerusalem, Herod was forced to flee with his family to a desert fortress on the plateau of Masada. He left his family there and set out for Rome to ask for help from Marc Antony. He was allowed to plead his case before the Senate in Rome, a combination of lawmakers and powerful citizens of Rome. When the Senate heard about Antigonus's alliance to the Parthians, they awarded Herod the throne of Judea.

HEROD THE KING

Herod had become king of the Jews in title. But while he was in Rome, Antigonus captured Herod's eldest brother, Phasael, and Hyrcanus. Rather than submit to the humiliation of prison or torture, Phasael smashed his head against his prison wall until he fell

Herod left his family at the rocky plateau of Masada and went to Rome to get support. Beyond the plateau lies the Dead Sea.

dead. Hyrcanus did not escape so easily. Antigonus cut off his ears, then sold him to the Parthians. The earless high priest became a captive and war trophy in Parthia.

Herod returned to Judea in 39 B.C. with an army of paid soldiers and Roman legions. Jews were unlikely to fight loyally for Herod, so he hired Arabs, Romans, Greeks, and even Germanic tribesmen from central Europe to fight. First he freed the fortress of Masada, where his family was being besieged. Then he swept through Judea, driving Antigonus's forces before him. He laid siege to Jerusalem. Antigonus's men defended the city against Herod and the Roman soldiers in many bloody battles, and the dead began to pile up outside Jerusalem's walls. In the end, though, Antigonus's forces weakened and Herod entered Jerusalem in triumph.

Roman soldiers began looting Jerusalem after Herod appealed to Rome to help him retake the city. Eventually Herod had to pay them to stop. This sculpture shows Roman soldiers removing loot from Jerusalem, in this case after Titus invaded the city—and destroyed the Temple begun by Herod—in A.D. 70. The sculpture is in the passageway of an arch in honor of Titus.

It was the custom of Roman soldiers to loot a fallen city. From Jerusalem they took gold, jewels, clothing, and women. But Herod did not want the Romans to take everything from Jerusalem. He asked the Roman commander if he was going to wind up being king over a desert. After all, if the Romans looted everything, then what would Herod have left to rule? To stop the looting, he agreed to pay the Romans out of his own riches.

The Romans turned to Antigonus to satisfy their bloodlust. They strung him up on a cross, where he was whipped and beheaded. Antigonus's death left Herod in full control of Jerusalem. He took the throne that the Romans had granted him earlier in Rome. Now he was king of the Jews in Judea both in title and in reality.

3

THE DESPISED DESPOT

Herod began his position on the Judean throne with an act of revenge. Remembering how the Sanhedrin had condemned his actions during the revolt in Galilee, Herod ordered his soldiers to slay forty-five of the seventy-one judges. He replaced the murdered judges with forty-five loyal supporters. With the court stacked to his advantage, Herod turned to the problem of finding a new high priest. Earless Hyrcanus, the old high priest, was still being held captive in Parthia.

Mariamme, Herod's wife, had a brother named Aristobulus (not to be confused with Herod's son, who was also named Aristobulus). He was the youngest surviving Hasmonean. Therefore, he was next in line

Herod the Great, king of Judea

for the office of high priest. After much hesitation, Herod appointed Aristobulus to this position.

THE DEATH OF A HIGH PRIEST

The Judean people quickly become attached to Aristobulus, and Herod realized that he had made a big mistake. Though Aristobulus was only about eighteen years old, he was becoming very influential. As a rightful Hasmonean prince, he was a threat to Herod's rule in Judea.

Herod realized he needed to get rid of Aristobulus. He invited the high priest to a day of relaxation at a shady oasis. There Herod's attendants splashed around in a pool of water, playing games and laughing. Young Aristobulus joined the revelers. They began pushing each other under the water in a playful manner. No one thought it was suspicious when they did the same to Aristobulus. However, when the high priest popped up to the water's surface, he was dead. Herod's men had held him under water until he had drowned.

ALEXANDRA'S HATRED

The Judeans wept bitterly at the death of the high priest. Herod claimed that Aristobulus's death was an accident, but Aristobulus's mother, Alexandra, and others suspected that he was responsible for the murder. To the Hasmoneans, it was another case of an Arab outsider trampling on their rights and traditions.

Alexandra had been against the marriage of Mariamme and Herod from the outset. She had always tried to turn Mariamme against him. She would whisper warnings into her daughter Mariamme's ear,

such as, "Always remember that you are a Hasmonean, while he is an Arab." Alexandra's hatred for Herod drove her to seek the help of the Egyptian queen, Cleopatra. Cleopatra showed Alexandra much sympathy. She pledged to do what she could to rid Judea of Herod.

Herod relied on an intricate system of spies to protect him from the plots of his enemies. Agents listened for treasonous talk amidst the chatter of the marketplaces and public baths. Before Alexandra and Cleopatra could do anything to Herod, his spies discovered their plans and exposed them. Herod openly accused Alexandra of plotting against him. The charge was true, of course, but little came of it. Alexandra attempted to escape from Jerusalem by hiding

Cleopatra receives Antony in pomp and splendor at the Egyptian Royal Palace in Alexandria, Egypt. As a descendant of one of Alexander the Great's generals, Cleopatra wanted to regain the greatness that the Greeks once had in the Mediterranean. Although Antony liked Herod, Cleopatra's sympathy with Alexandra, Mariamme's mother, was a constant threat to Herod and his alliance with Antony.

in a coffin. Herod's spies uncovered this trick, too. He made Alexandra look a fool by publicly revealing Alexandra in the coffin trying to flee.

ANTONY AND CLEOPATRA

Meanwhile, Cleopatra's attentions were being drawn elsewhere. She was the favorite of Marc Antony, who was said to be under her spell. Some said Cleopatra was causing him to ignore his responsibilities in Rome. The Roman people were turning against him while he stayed with Cleopatra in the lap of luxury at Alexandria, Egypt's capital.

Cleopatra and Antony dreamed of supreme control of Rome. The two planned to defeat Octavius, who was the commander of the western half of Rome's territory, and move the capital from Rome to Alexandria.

Antony called upon all of his allies in the east to fight Octavius. Herod was too busy fighting neighboring Arabs to participate. He thereby escaped the defeat Antony and Cleopatra suffered off the coast of Greece in the Battle of Actium in 31 B.C. Octavius had triumphed. Even before Antony was captured, Herod took an oath of allegiance to Octavius. Herod had learned from his father the necessity of preserving alliances with Rome, no matter who its leader was. By this method he was able to rule over a nation that hated him.

4

THE GRAECO-ROMAN BUILDER

That history should call Herod "Great" reflects his powerful impact on Judea, not the merits of his character. He came to be known as Herod the Great partly to distinguish him from his sons, some of whom were also named Herod. But he was also called "Great" because he was a great builder. When he died, in 4 B.C., the hills and plains of Judea were dotted with his cities and fortresses. Ships sailed in and out of his great port of Caesarea. And the great Temple at Jerusalem, a project that Herod had begun fifteen years earlier, was still under construction.

After first becoming king of Judea with the help of Antony, Herod converted an old Jewish fortress on

*The geographical location of Jerusalem offered little comfort
to its people. It was hewn from an inhospitable land where
water and arable soil were in short supply. The life-giving force
of Jerusalem has always been faith, and it is an important
spiritual center for Christians and Muslims as well as Jews.*

top of Temple hill in Jerusalem into his palace. It towered above Judea. It gave him a view of the city and protected him from attack. He named his new palace the Antonia, in honor of Marc Antony.

MARIAMME'S PLOT

When Octavius defeated Antony and Cleopatra, Herod sailed to meet him at the Mediterranean island of Rhodes. He wanted to congratulate Octavius and win his favor with expensive gifts. Before leaving, he had sent Alexandra and Mariamme to the city of Alexandrium to await his return. But while Herod was flattering Octavius in Rhodes, Mariamme was making a plan to poison him upon his return.

Pleased with Herod's show of loyalty, Octavius gave him rule over some territory surrounding Judea. When Herod returned to Judea, his spies told him of Mariamme's plot. He put Mariamme on trial, and the judges found her guilty. Herod ordered her death.

The decision to kill Mariamme drove Herod to the edge of madness, for he still loved her. Racked by fever and chills, he would wake in the night screaming her name, while his frightened servants looked on.

Alexandra had now lost both her son and daughter to Herod's cruelty. She hated him more than ever. She hoped that he would not recover from his madness, and she tried to turn the people against him

while he lay ill. But Herod's sickness faded. Finally, to be rid of his mother-in-law, he ordered her death as well.

The executions of Mariamme and Alexandra drove the Judeans farther from Herod. He now ruled only through force and by the will of Octavius. In 27 B.C. Octavius proclaimed himself emperor of all the Roman provinces. To celebrate the occasion, he took the name Augustus Caesar.

THE SPELL OF HELLENISM

To commemorate Octavius's victory four years earlier at Actium, Herod organized the Actian Games. These Graeco-Roman entertainments included wrestling, chariot racing, and musical competitions, and were held every five years. Herod had a large arena built for the games that bore inscriptions praising Augustus.

The Actian Games probably upset the Jews for sev-

A stern and vengeful Mariamme appears to Herod as a ghost after her murder. The death of Mariamme, of all Herod's crimes, seems to have haunted him most.

eral reasons. The racing chariots were symbols of war, specifically the conquest of Judea by foreigners. Also, the Greek-style musical competitions and theatrical performances contained a lot of bawdy Greek humor, which would upset Orthodox Jewish morals. Despite some protests, though, the games were a big success, and many Jews won prizes in the competitions.

Herod was under the spell of Greek culture, known as Hellenism. The Actian Games reflected these Hellenistic traits. Surely, he must have thought, this was the height of ancient civilization: feasting and drinking while watching Greek games in a stately public building. Herod inherited from the Greeks and Romans a love for the construction of splendid buildings that would promote his greatness by their grandeur. His palace, the Antonia (the one he named

The simplicity and endurance of Roman architecture is still marveled at today. The perfect symmetry of the arch, both elegant and durable, can be seen in the foundations of many Roman constructions such as this aqueduct leading to Caesarea, which was the center of Roman administration in Judea.

after Marc Antony), was an example of this Graeco-Roman style.

This Greek influence had swept the area after the death of Alexander the Great in 323 B.C. Alexander was the champion of the ancient Greeks. After defeating the Persian Empire, which had long threatened Greece, Alexander marched all the way to India. He spread Greek customs and tastes throughout the East. By Herod's time, the government at Rome had risen while Greek influence had declined, but the Romans imitated the Greeks in many ways.

Many of Herod's building projects reflected this influence. He rebuilt a seaport city known as Strato's Tower and renamed it Caesarea, in honor of Augustus

The western gate of Sebaste, built by Herod. Because of strict Jewish laws regarding the worshipping of an image, King Herod could not even put his likeness on a coin. Instead, he satisfied his passion for public recognition through his grand building projects. The Roman historian Suetonius said that Augustus "found Rome brick and left it marble." Herod wanted to do the same for the cities of Judea.

Caesar (Octavius). He fortified the ancient city of Samaria, which he renamed Sebaste (a Greek translation of the name Augustus). Herod's Graeco-Roman buildings stood as a constant reminder to the people of Judea of his allegiance to Rome.

AID TO JUDEA

Despite his fanatical devotion to Rome, Herod was not entirely cold to the Jews. In 25 B.C. the farmlands of Judea began to dry up, eventually causing a serious famine. The year's crop withered completely, so that not even the seeds could be used for planting the following year. Herod acted swiftly. He collected money, gained in part by melting down his own precious statuary, jewelry, and silver and gold plates,

The Wailing Wall is all that remains of the Temple at Jerusalem built by Herod. It is now a part of the wall that surrounds the Dome of the Rock. The enormity of the wall conveys a sense of how spectacular the temple must have been. People place written prayers in the little crevices, or whisper prayers into them.

and bought grain in Egypt. Soldiers distributed the food, while bakers were brought in to cook for the sick and elderly. Herod even provided seeds to be planted for the next year's crops.

Even though Herod was never very interested in the traditional religion of the Jews, he decided to rebuild the Temple of Jerusalem at his own expense. He wanted to recall the grandeur of the Temple of Solomon, which the Babylonians had destroyed in 586 B.C. He also hoped to win support from the Jews by restoring the Temple. Herod employed one thousand priests to rebuild this sacred place. Thousands of other craftsmen built the outer structures. The work began around the year 19 B.C.

The reconstruction of the Temple was certainly Herod's most ambitious project. In 10 B.C. he marked the completion of the Temple with the slaughter of hundreds of oxen and a great celebration. But construction continued on the outer structures even after Herod's death. Despite their hatred for Herod, the Jews recorded in their sacred writing the magnificence of his rebuilding of the Temple. They wrote, "He who never saw Herod's edifice has never in his life seen a beautiful building."

5

THE DEADLY PATRIARCH

Though in awe of Herod's Temple project, the Judeans could not forget his past injustices or ignore his continuing cruelties. So the reconstruction of the Temple failed to win support among the Judeans. Beyond Judea, however, Herod won some fame among Jewish communities. These people were not directly affected by his cruelty, and they benefited from his fatherly gestures.

When the Babylonians invaded Judea and destroyed the first Temple, many Jews went into exile. This scattering of the Jews is known as the Diaspora. Herod already had relations with diaspora Jews in Egypt. When he sailed to Asia Minor (modern Turkey)

Herod's hill-top palace once rose above the stretches of the Judean Desert. The remains of these stone columns are situated in an elegant courtyard leading up to a synagogue.

to meet the Roman commander Agrippa, he encountered more diaspora communities.

HELPING THE DIASPORA JEWS

Agrippa was Augustus's son-in-law, and chief naval commander at the Battle of Actium. Herod knew the value of flattering someone so close to the emperor. He soon found himself, however, appealing to Agrippa to better the position of the Jews in Asia Minor. They were forced to serve in the Roman military, despite religious teachings against such service. And Herod discovered that the money the Jews sent to Judea as donations to the Temple was being stolen.

Agrippa listened to Herod's pleas and excused the Jews from military duty. He also granted them protection under Roman law. In this manner Herod earned a reputation as a protector of the diaspora Jews. However, while Herod was away in Asia Minor, events in Judea began to turn against him.

SONS AGAINST THEIR FATHER

Alexander and Aristobulus, Herod's sons by Mariamme, had returned from Rome, where they had learned the importance of their royal blood. The sons quickly became advocates of Hasmonean rule and said openly that Herod was unworthy of the Judean

Coins bore this likeness of Agrippa. Coins in antiquity were not only money but also propaganda advertising the character and deeds of a statesman.

throne. They also hated their father for killing their mother. So Herod soon found himself opposed by a new generation of Hasmoneans—but these Hasmoneans were his own sons.

Herod attempted to frighten Alexander and Aristobulus by bringing formal accusations against them before Augustus in 12 B.C. As Herod acted the injured father and Alexander and Aristobulus acted the innocent sons, Augustus watched with disgust. What kind of king, he wondered, could not even rule his sons? The trial amounted to little. Augustus dismissed all of them after Herod and his sons promised to patch things up.

FINAL REVENGE

Herod returned to Judea, no better off than before. Since his sons by Mariamme had turned against him, Herod summoned Antipater. Antipater, his son by Doris, whom he had previously kept in the background, now became his favorite and heir to the throne. Herod assumed that he was bringing an ally to court. But Antipater also entered into the plots against him. After all, the sooner Herod died, the sooner Antipater would be king.

Meanwhile, Alexander and Aristobulus were in a desperate struggle to get rid of Herod and Antipater. Plots were hatched and plots were uncovered. Herod again asked Augustus for help. Augustus seemed to take the accusations more seriously the second time. He granted Herod the right of patriarchy, which, by Roman law, allowed Herod to kill his sons. About 7 B.C. Herod's judges found Alexander and Aristobulus guilty of treason, and they were executed by strangulation. Restlessness bubbled up from the depths of Judea. People became resentful as they watched Herod execute generation after generation of Hasmonean royals.

MADNESS AND DEATH

As the Judeans became upset over the deaths of Herod's sons, Herod became ill. No one knows exactly what afflicted him. The Jewish historian Josephus describes Herod suffering from uncontrollable itching, coughing, fever, and worms. His body was deteriorating, but his illness may have been psychological as well. The madness and nightmares he experienced after executing his wife Mariamme may have returned. Herod had now murdered most of his family and earned the hatred of his subjects.

He was a man entirely alone. His frail body was barely able to support his last fits of rage and the weight of a lifetime of abominable cruelties. It was in this state of depravity, near the end of his life, that he may have directed the Slaughter of the Innocents.

The feared standard of Imperial Rome. It bears the inscription S. P. Q. R., which stands for the Latin Senatus Populusque Romanus—*the Senate and Roman People.*

Antipater plotted with Herod's last surviving brother, Pheroras, to quicken the king's death. Herod's subjects began to rebel. His spies learned of the new treacheries, and he roused himself to a few last acts of cruelty. But as he became more ill, he lost his resolve and became more and more confused. He changed his will three times, finally disinheriting Antipater.

One of Herod's last acts was to affix a golden eagle, the symbol of Imperial Rome, above the main gate of the Temple of Jerusalem. The eagle was extremely offensive to the Jews, for it polluted the holy temple with a foreign symbol and reminded them of Herod's cruelty. Two rabbis organized a party of eager youths to cut down the hated symbol. In broad daylight the bird was hacked off with axes. For their offense, the two rabbis and their followers were burned alive while Herod, sick and dying, lay on a couch and watched.

In 4 B.C. Herod had Antipater poisoned, and many of the religious leaders who openly rebelled were burned alive. Pheroras escaped Herod's wrath only by dying a natural death before the king could reach him. Herod himself tried to commit suicide but failed. Then, only five days after Antipater's death, Herod developed a terrible fever and fell dead.

When King Herod died, Imperial Rome swooped down on Jerusalem, and in the year A.D. 6 Judea became a Roman province. The Jews hated Herod so much that they themselves asked Rome to occupy Judea, in order to prevent Herod's surviving sons from ruling in his name. In their anger and fear, the Jews, as Herod had once done, looked to Rome. But the Jews did so only to substitute one master for another.

If the Jews wept at the passing of Herod, it was for

*A rolling stone blocks the entrance to the "Tomb of Herod."
The sepulchre is probably the burial place of Mariamme and
possibly of Herod Agrippa, the grandson of Herod the Great.*

joy. They were finally rid of a ferocious tyrant. Nonetheless, Herod was buried in stately fashion, as described by Josephus:

There was a solid gold bier, adorned with precious stones and draped with the richest purple. On it lay the body wrapped in crimson, with a diadem on the head and above that a golden crown, and the sceptre by the right hand. The bier was escorted by Herod's sons and the whole body of his kinsmen, followed by his Spearmen, the Thracian Company, and his Germans and Gauls, all in full battle order, headed by their commanders and all the officers, and followed by five hundred freedmen carrying spices.

TIMELINE

134–104 B.C.	John Hyrcanus rules as Hasmonean King and high priest; Jews conquer Edom
76 B.C.	Hasmonean King Alexander Jannaeus dies, sons wage civil war for power in Judea
c. 74 B.C.	Herod born
63 B.C.	Roman general Pompey enters Jerusalem, ends Judean civil war
48 B.C.	Caesar defeats Pompey at Pharsalus; Pompey murdered in Egypt
47 B.C.	Herod appointed governor of Galilee by his father, Antipater
44 B.C.	Julius Caesar assassinated
43 B.C.	Antipater assassinated, Herod becomes governor of Judea
41 B.C.	Herod allies himself with Marc Antony
40 B.C.	Parthians invade Syria; Herod flees to Masada with family
39 B.C.	Roman Senate appoints Herod King of Judea; Herod drives Antigonus out of Judea, enters Jerusalem
31 B.C.	Octavius defeats Antony at Actium, then confirms Herod's rule of Judea
27 B.C.	Herod conducts Actian Games in honor of Octavius's victory over Antony; Octavius declares himself Augustus Caesar, first Roman emperor
25 B.C.	Drought in Judea; Herod collects money to buy grain from Egypt
25–13 B.C.	Herod oversees building of Caesarea, Sebaste, fortresses, theaters, and other public buildings
19 B.C.	Reconstruction of Temple of Jerusalem begins
12 B.C.	Herod brings accusations against his sons, Alexander and Aristobulus, before Roman court; Augustus (Octavius) dismisses charges
7 B.C.	Alexander and Aristobulus found guilty of treason by Judean judges and executed
6 B.C.	Herod becomes ill
4 B.C.	Herod orders the death of his son Antipater; Herod dies five days later
A.D. 6	Judea becomes a Roman province

FOR MORE INFORMATION

FOR FURTHER READING

Corbishley, Mike. *Everyday Life in Roman Times*. New York: Franklin Watts, 1994.

Goldwurm, Hersh, and Meir Holder. *History of the Jewish People, Vol. 1: The Second Temple Era*. Brooklyn, NY: Mesorah Publishers, 1993.

Poulton, Michael. *Augustus and the Ancient Romans*. Chatham, NJ: Raintree Steck-Vaughn, 1992.

Rosenfield, Geraldine. *The Heroes of Masada*. New York: United Synagogue of America Books.

FOR ADVANCED READERS

Brauer, George C. *Judea Weeping: The Jewish Struggle Against Rome from Pompey to Masada, 63 B.C. to A.D. 73*. New York: Thomas Y. Crowell, 1970.

Josephus. *The Jewish War*. Translated by G. A. Williamson. New York: Penguin Books, 1959.

Sandmel, Samuel. *Herod: Portrait of a Tyrant*. New York: Lippincott, 1967.

Tamarin, Alfred H. *Revolt in Judea: The Road to Masada*. New York: Four Winds Press, 1968.

INTERNET SITES

Home pages and directories will link you to a myriad of Web sites about the ancient Mediterranean world:

Exploring Ancient World Cultures (University of Evansville):
    http://cedar.evansville.edu/~wcweb/wc101/
ArchNet (University of Connecticut):
    http://spirit.lib.uconn.edu/archaeology.html
ROMARCH, a home page on archaeology in Italy and the
    Roman provinces:
    http://personal-www.umich.edu/~pfoss/ROMARCH.html
The Ancient World Web:
    http://atlantic.evsc.virginia.edu/julia/AncientWorld.html

One example of the many sites you can visit is *Art and Architectural Sculpture of the Mediterranean Basin*: http//www.ncsa. uiuc.edu/SDG/Experimental/anu-art-history/architecture.html

INDEX

Page numbers in *italics* refer to illustrations

ABOUT THE AUTHOR

Robert Green is a freelance writer who lives in New York City. He holds a B.A. in English literature from Boston University and is the author of *"Vive la France": The French Resistance during World War II* (Franklin Watts). He has also written biographies of three other important figures of the ancient world: *Alexander the Great, Cleopatra,* and *Tutankhamun.*